# Geriatric Nostalgia

# Geriatric Nostalgia

**Amusing and Uplifting Poems
about old age & life in general**

by **Sheila Keen**

**Signed Illustrations by Bill Downing**

Sheila Keen first started writing amusing and uplifting poetry to make friends and neighbours laugh after she moved with her husband into their retirement apartment on Cowes seafront.

Since then she has had various poems published in the popular women's magazines

Sheila has supported the RSPCA on the Isle of Wight for many years. In the past, she helped set up and run a Charity Shop for them in Ventnor and she now makes greeting cards to raise money for the charity.

This book is helping them too, as Sheila is donating £1 to the RSPCA at Godshill on the Isle of Wight for every copy sold.

**This book is dedicated to
my dear late husband Alec**

With grateful thanks to
Sue, Ian, Andy, Caron,
Jan, Steve, Diana, Bill and Cherry

# Nostalgia, Memories & Old Age

# Getting Old & Miserable – Not us!

We start the day with aches and pains,
in misery we wallow.
The curtains drawn, we see the dawn,
A pretty sky will follow.

It really is a lovely day,
the birds begin to sing.
The Winter's gone, the frosts away,
we're going into Spring.

When in our younger days we worked,
we had no time to stare.
We rushed around and never shirked,
no time to be aware.

Now in our twilight years we find,
that benefits are present.
Time to talk, and help – be kind,
life really is quite pleasant.

Enjoy the time to chat awhile,
the hardest bit is done.
So laugh and joke to raise a smile,
It's time to have some fun!

## The Horrors of Old Age

The hairs on my head,
are getting very thin.
They have all decided to grow,
upon my chin.

I pounce upon the tweezers,
get more light.
I swear they've grown at least,
one inch overnight.

With tweezers at the ready,
I try to pluck.
But find it's disappeared for now,
just my luck.

My cat's got whiskers,
that's alright.
But on grandma's double chin,
it's not a pretty sight.

# It's That Time of Year Again

Queues in the street,
what can it be?
Lots of senior citizens,
something's going free!

War time habits
cling on hard.
But surely nothing's rationed,
I haven't got a card.

I'll ask this pleasant lady,
she's got a lovely smile.
I'll have to push my way up here,
and up the middle aisle.

Could you tell me what's amiss,
and what's all this to-do?
Why yes, she said, don't you know,
its jab time for the Flu!

# Lovely Uncomplicated Old Age

I wake up in the morning,
I'm glad to have my wits.
I grab the morning paper,
I'm not in the OBITS!

I waggle all my tootsies,
making sure the joints are free.
And apply the embrocation,
to my stiff and painful knee.

When I've had my breakfast,
I think I'll have a walk.
I'll meet up with some schoolfriends,
we'll reminisce and talk.

It's not easy to remember
everybody's name.
But colours I can recognize,
upon their walking frame.

We're happy with our memories,
we seldom ever moan.
We're glad that we're so active,
and know we're not alone.

I push my useful walking aid,
along the busy street.
As homeward bound I'm going,
never knowing who I'll meet.

I've had a pleasant morning,
with a positive thinking bunch.
My spirits have been lifted,
so now I'll have some lunch.

## Childhood Memories

Gobstoppers, Lucky Bags and Sherbet Dabs.
Days by the seaside, looking for crabs.

A day in the country was every child's dream.
Where the clear spring water formed a trickling stream.

Then it was 'off with our shoes' as we dangled our toes,
and with jam jar and string, we'd fish for minnows.

The slippery stepping-stones were quite scary,
trying not to fall in, one would have to be wary.

The picnic was of course the great treat,
with lots of special things brought for us to eat.

When eating was done, we'd play chasing & hide,
behind massive trees in the lush countryside.

The picnic box was then packed away,
as homeward we'd travel re-living the day.

Just one more treat for today it would seem.
We would stop at the van for a penny ice-cream.

# Geriatrica

I never thought that at this stage,
I'd find the benefits of old age.
Some things I can't do, never mind,
but lots I can do, and I find
that small achievements mean a lot,
does it matter that word I forgot?

The pleasure a friendly word can give,
our happiest memories we try to re-live.
The warmth of the sun on an aching knee,
the flower that attracts a big bumblebee.
We've time to stand and be aware,
of gentle breezes and balmy air.

When young, no time to look around,
each day new challenges abound.
Now safely in my soft cocoon,
**"GERIATRICA"** is quite a boon.
So, if contentment I can't hide,
Old Age has made me satisfied.

# Nothing's Perfect!

After swallowing a dose of pride,
a Hearing Aid I got.
It fits quite neatly right inside,
and helps me quite a lot.

But sadly nothing's perfect,
and mixing in a crowd,
I can hear the person near,
but surrounding noise is far too loud.

So we're not deaf, we're in denial
to important meetings we shall go,
only to find that after a while
a voice in my ear says, Battery Low.

My teeth were nice and even,
I liked them quite a lot.
But many years of chewing,
some are crumbling, some have rot.

A visit to the Dentist,
before it's all too late.
Dentist says, I'll put new teeth
upon a dental plate.

But I'm frightened to cough,
or sneeze, or shout.
For if I do,
my teeth fly out.

I feel unsteady, never quick,
they all suggest I use a stick.
It seemed a sensible idea,
t'will take away the family's fear.

I speed around the local shop
confident in myself.
But at the checkout I did stop,
I'd left my stick upon the shelf.

The staff all searched, and then they found
my nice new stick upon the ground.
We find a dozen sticks each week.
They're in that cupboard, take a peek.

Spare parts are not perfect we will find,
the inventors have all been very kind.
We're lucky to have them and I pray,
that I'll use these 'spare parts' for many a day.

# Grandma's Washing Day

Grandma's laundry was a washtub and a mangle.
A scrubbing brush and dolly blue,
was all that she could wangle.

Grandma didn't have a modern tumble drier,
sheets went through the mangle,
and were dried by the fire.

Today's fire restrictions did not apply,
so common sense was used
until they were dry.

They dried outside if weather was fine,
hung up with Dolly Pegs
upon a washing line.

The house would be steamy and smell of soap,
nobody complained
as it was full of love and hope.

The copper and the mangle would be put away,
And the flat iron would be used
the following day.

# Covid — Here We Go Again

Once more in demand,
toilet rolls and flour.
The rules for beating Covid,
changes from hour to hour.
Ten o'clock closing time,
for bars and clubs.
Masks must be worn,
in transport, shops and pubs.

Many senior citizens,
show signs of stress.
Continuous isolation,
puts their brain power in a mess.
To get through this,
we'll need to all be saints.
Adding agoraphobia,
to the OAP's complaints.

When finally we emerge,
and it's safe to mix.
We've lost our art of shopping,
as our memory plays tricks.
We've lines across our faces,
Are they worry lines, I ask?
Oh no, that's a relief,
just the imprint of my mask!

## Pros and Cons of Ageing

Warts and moles - annoying tags.
Muscles weaken - bosom sags!

Gums shrink back - what have I got?
A mouth which holds a lot of pot!

My knees are weak - what can I do?
I have three legs - instead of two.

My hearing's gone - but does it matter?
I don't hear swearing, noise and clatter.

Head feels heavy - shoulder's droop,
I never thought I'd start to stoop.

I can no longer touch my toes,
But still write poems - still write prose.

I've time for hobbies - join some clubs.
Enjoy my garden, flowers and shrubs.

I've found new interests - made new friends.
The benefits of retirement never ends.

I'm living life at a different pace.
Peace and tranquillity, I've time to embrace.

I've even time to stop and chat.
Time to enjoy my retirement flat.

My wrinkles are now called laughter lines.
My scribbled doodles - new designs!

When conversing and can't find a word,
it's aggravating and it's quite absurd.

But now I think I can't be perfect,
so say my pause is for effect.

I like to reminisce and nap,
and don't find age a handicap!

# Wartime Shortages

Now halfway through my 90th year,
memories I have – quite a lot.
The visions of some are still very clear,
others I've clearly forgot!

### Childhood
Our milk was delivered by pony and cart.
Hooked on the churn, a pint measure.
The horse knew the round, when to stop, when to start.
To see him was always a pleasure.

### Wartime
Mashed parsnip sandwiches – banana so we thought,
set upon the table in wartime greyish bread.
Dried egg and sausages sometimes could be bought.
Birthday cake, no icing, had cardboard tops instead.

### Teens

Gravy browning tanned our legs,
we thought it was a hoot.
Pencilled seams were all the rage,
we really looked the part.
Who could guess our undies,
were made from parachute.
We stretched our clothing coupons,
it was a work of art.

### Present

Childhood memories are all very well,
it's in the present that I live.
So in the past I must not dwell,
but see what pleasure I can give.
I have imagination, my humour, and my brain.
I'll use those gifts. I can. I know it.
Negative thoughts are all in vain,
I think perhaps I'll be a **Poet!**

## Oldies Social Whirl

My friend Rita, asked me out for tea.
So I looked at the diary to see
which day was free.

**Monday** -The Dentist...
check-up time again.

**Tuesday** - My Tootsies...
before they cause me pain.

**Wednesday** - The Groceries...
delivered every week.

**Thursday** - My Hearing-Aid...
which started to squeak.

**Friday** - Mobility Scooter needs a service...
the battery keeps running down makes me nervous.


Oh joy! The weekend is entirely free.
Two days of heaven, JUST FOR ME!

## Old Values

Would I like to be young again?
To that I say - definitely not.
We may be doddery and sometimes in pain,
we're not tempted by "bingeing and pot."

We were taught to say, thank you & please.
We gave up our seat on a bus.
A warning glance would make us freeze,
we weren't allowed to make a fuss.

Our elders were always given respect,
our guidelines we wouldn't dare cross.
Good manners we would never neglect,
we knew our parents were always The Boss.

Young people these days are ruled by the net,
to their families they never converse.
How can they discuss the problems they get?
Without help, they will only get worse.

So no, I'm happy with life at this stage,
the generation gap is too wide.
I understand folk of a similar age,
but modern life, I can't abide.

## Grains of Sand

I have never in my lifetime,
met anyone I knew,
from school, career, or commerce.
I've known thousands – not a few.

Do we really make a difference
to the progress of this land.
Or are we all too busy
burying our heads in the sand?

We share sunshine in the summer,
and evenings balmy air.
But do we really take the time
to look around and be aware?

The lonely and the elderly
would love to shake your hand.
And not just be considered,
another grain of sand.

# Getting Old?

I went upstairs to get a pen,
to write my shopping list.
I looked around and wondered when,
I had become so ageist.


Who were these folk whilst getting old,
moaned about their plight.
'I can't see this,' or so I'm told,
'I cannot sleep at night.'


I boil the kettle, make some tea,
the ironing I will fold.
My hip is hurting, so's my knee,
Oh dear, I'm getting old

## Wartime Memories

A favourite walk down Lover's Lane,
where couples went to court.
With bramble in the hedgerows,
where tasty treats were sought.


Whilst walking there one autumn day,
a horse and cart went by.
The farmer's boy, he raised his cap,
with a grin he winked his eye.

As he drove his cart away,
my eye fell on the ground.
A swede had toppled from his load,
it hadn't made a sound.

He surely wouldn't miss it,
to me it was a meal.
I picked it up and wiped it off,
I didn't mean to steal.

With potato and an Oxo cube,
it was a meal for two.
With the addition of an onion,
it made a meatless stew.

With rationing and shortages,
we used everyday resources.
While all the men were absent,
as they'd gone to join the forces.

As I look back and reminisce,
I gratefully give thanks.
That life is much more peaceful now,
not full of bombs and tanks.

## Morning Sounds!

I wake up in the morning,
and once the bed is made.
I finish in the bathroom,
and grab my hearing aid.

I draw back the curtains,
I can hear that gentle **swish.**
The sunrise is so beautiful,
for more I could not wish.

I go into the kitchen,
I can hear the kettle **sing.**
I can put on my porridge,
as I'll hear the timer **ping.**

Sitting having breakfast,
my friendly clock goes **tick.**
Then I hear the postman,
as the letterbox goes **click.**

The Woodpecker is out there **tapping,**
at his favourite tree.
I can hear the morning chorus,
and the **humming** of a bee.

I can hear the gentle **trickle,**
of a nearby waterfall.
And the blackbird and the robin,
to their mates they softly call.

If I can't stand the traffic noise,
and when people bawl and **shout.**
I always have the option,
**my hearing aid comes out**.

## A Hairy Problem

My hair was once my crowning glory,
curly, thick and black.
This is a familiar old age story,
no sense in looking back.

I try to always look my best,
with co-ordinated dress.
I'm facing life with lots of zest,
I still like to impress.

The problem now is thinning hair.
The challenge here is big.
Is there an answer?  Would I dare?
I'll go and buy a wig.

The heat in summer - winter wind,
the weather's never right.
I've had to learn to be thick-skinned,
till I take it off at night!

# Dining Out

We're dining out at our favourite venue,
dressed in our smartest attire.
The waiter brings a tempting menu,
lots of dishes for us to admire.

Condiments arriving next of course,
all set on a silver tray.
Mayonnaise, tomato and tartare sauce,
a wonderful tasty array.

Someone there must know the trick,
of opening these packs.
There's supposed to be a little nick,
which clearly this one lacks.

I ask the waiter standing by,
if he would lend a hand.
He nods politely, 'I will try.
These packets I can never understand.'

Just then it opens with a spurt.
Sauce flies across the table.
He says, 'Don't worry, no one's hurt.'
As polite as he is able.

Why don't they realise ageing joints
are just not strong enough,
to tear plastic packs at designated points,
and provide us with the bottled stuff.

The meal was great, the service too.
We enjoyed our birthday treat.
Next year we'll avoid all this to-do,
and stay at home to eat.

# The Wonders of Nature

# Retirement Life Is Not So Bad

When we came to Briary Court,
we left our friends behind.
The furry and the feathered sort,
we didn't think they'd mind.

Our neighbours said that they would feed,
our regular dependants.
And see to all their daily needs,
to keep their feathers all resplendent.

Now we have a different bunch,
to visit daily for their lunch.
We spread the food upon the ground,
where pigeons, crows and gulls abound.

Blue tits come from far and wide,
to see if we've put nuts inside
their feeder hanging on the wall,
then to their friends they softly call,
It's full, come down, we'll have a ball.
There's plenty here to feed us all.

The pied wagtail flew in today,
and woodpecker with his coat so gay.
He's there with coloured friend the jay,
I hope they all decide to stay.

While sitting on our garden seat,
red squirrels feed around our feet.
The tiny field mice eat the bread,
ground feeders o'er the ground have spread.

But the thing that really makes our day,
is to watch the little fox cubs play.
So moving wasn't quite so bad,
There's wildlife here at our new pad.

## The Sea Has Its Uses

The lapping of the waves,
as they hit the sandy shore.
And trickle into caves,
where children will explore.

The tide takes people unaware,
the pebbles it will polish.
The children's castles built with care,
the sea will then demolish.

Some crabs beneath the rocks have hid,
waiting for that tide.
To take them back into the sea,
where they no longer need to hide.

The waves come in, and then recede,
it happens every day.
They bring in flotsam and seaweed,
then take it all away.

For children love the seaside,
filling buckets to the brim.
They can run and play and hide,
and even learn to swim.

## Busy Fairies

There are fairies in my garden,
it's very plain to see.
And all of them are artists,
they're as busy as can be.

Some of them work daytime,
some throughout the night.
Some work with darker colours,
some extremely bright.

Some fairies paint the finest lines,
others paint the dots.
In spring the yellow daffodils,
and blue forget-me-nots.

The roses in the summer,
with all those shades of pink.
Who has the job of scenting them,
The fairies – don't you think?

There are fairies in my garden,
although they are not seen.
Who has the largest paintbox,
with all those shades of green.

I think they have some helpers,
the butterflies and bees.
Which fly amongst the flowers,
And pollinate with ease.

To the fairies in my garden,
who are working all this magic.
I say, please stay – don't go away,
for I'd find that really tragic.

# An Annual Task

There's a chill in the air,
which says that Autumn is here.
Morning mists are present,
taking quite a while to clear.

When Autumn arrives,
there are lots of jobs to do.
And if you don't mind,
I will mention just a few.

The deadwood in the garden,
all needs shredding.
And the shrubs need cutting back,
a job I'm dreading.

The Autumn leaves are turning rust,
and are falling all around.
The compost heap needs emptying,
 and spreading on the ground.

The plant-pots all need washing,
and putting in the shed.
The squirrels are collecting nuts,
to store for weeks ahead.

The wind has brought the twigs down,
and made a lot of clutter.
I've got to get the ladders out,
to clear that dirty gutter.

The gardens are so enjoyable,
and this is all I ask,
that I can keep my health and strength,
to do this Annual Task.

## The Compost Heap

The compost heap was warm and deep,
as I dug the fork in hard.
The steam it rose and filled my nose,
as it drifted across the yard.

That lovely loam was someone's home,
as my joy had turned to guilt.
A toad hopped out, I heard it shout,
'There are babies in that silt.'

A slow worm slid from where it hid,
all glistening like a jewel.
As it slithered by, I heard it cry,
'I think you're very cruel.'

I'm in a state, the flowers can wait,
the wildlife must come first.
I'll get out the hose and spray that rose,
at least I'll quench its thirst.

As I walked away, 'we've won the day,'
a field mouse squeaked with glee.
'We've kept our home amongst the loam.'
Then he scampered up a tree.

## The Storm

**Swish** went the large magnolia tree,
as a stormy gust went by.
**Whoosh** went the graceful conifer,
I wish I'd not grown so high.

My cones have all dropped one by one,
my spines are hanging on.
But will look so bedraggled,
when this storm is gone.

My friend the holly tree close by
is sturdy – that is true.
But lots of scarlet berries
have diminished to a few.

Tomorrow could be nice and calm,
we could hear the robin sing.
And all the trees, now looking bare,
will get new leaves for Spring.

# A Gardener's Delight

The garden seat it beckons me
to have a little rest,
Just for sixty seconds,
I'll do my very best.

Have you ever known a gardener
sit for very long?
It's nice to hear the blackbirds
sing their pretty little song.

But there's work around the corner,
waiting to be done.
We really can't afford the time
for sitting in the sun.

The roses all need spraying,
there's greenfly and there's blight,
I swear that massive bindweed
wasn't there last night!

The secateurs go snipping,
butterflies abound,
and the scented rose petals
go floating to the ground.

I see the fuller picture
of all this fond attention,
which makes the garden beautiful,
a little I must mention.

The fuchsias and the sweet peas,
the colourful penstemon.
The dahlias and the sunflowers
are a lovely shade of lemon.

Delphiniums and campanulas,
a gorgeous show of blue.
While lupins tall, against the wall
seem every shade and hue.

We'll soon be in late summer,
with asters, golden rod,
and pink nerines in autumn,
with the grace of God.

I will sit down upon that seat,
to hear the Robin sing,
I'll look at gardening brochures,
I'm planning now for Spring!

# Happy Hour with Horace

Horace is my hose-pipe friend,
we meet each night at seven.
He helps me with the watering,
it's my idea of heaven.

The sun is cooling down,
it's the best time of the day.
The birdbath needs refilling,
must be done without delay.

Watering the garden,
to some might seem a chore.
Tranquillity takes over,
it's really not a bore.

The peace is unbelievable,
no voices to be heard.
Just rustling in the branches,
the night song of a bird.

I've turned off the hosepipe,
my flowers have had a drink.
I've had a peaceful hour,
to appreciate and think.

I'll walk around the garden,
and smell the scented air.
With time to stand and cogitate,
admire and be aware.

The beauty of a garden turns
despair into hope.
Bringing calmness to the troubled,
and helping them to cope.

My garden is to me,
the nearest thing to heaven.
I've got a rendezvous with Horace,
tomorrow night at seven.

# Summer Gardens

The beauty of our gardens
filled with summer flowers,
where we can sit admiring
them for many pleasant hours.

The different shades of roses,
fill the air with heady scent.
While the buddleia and the lavender
make all the bees content.

The fuchsias are amazing,
the gardens they enhance.
A little flutter of the wind
will make their flowers dance.

The gold and chocolate iris,
as its petals will enfold,
showing speckled marks, in lights and darks,
a treasure to behold.

The clematis and the sun flowers
are climbing up the wall.
While hollyhocks and scented stocks
are growing very tall.

The asters blue of every hue
and lovely golden rod,
will follow in the autumn,
with the grace of God.

Our flowers are therapeutic,
our troubled minds can calm.
Enjoy our Summer gardens,
they can heal our souls like balm.

## The Seasons

### Spring

The bare trees of the countryside,
show little tips of green.
And pussy willow catkins,
now can just be seen.

### Summer

Bright colours in the gardens,
the days are warm and long.
And the birds at last are singing,
their welcome tuneful song.

### Autumn

We see the autumn colours,
of orange, gold and rust.
And the falling leaves beneath our feet,
as we crush them into dust.

### Winter

The biting chill of winter,
the glistening on the snow,
as Jack Frost makes his patterns,
and indoor fires glow.

## The Stormy Sea

When storms are due, we know the signs.
The seagulls know it well.
They turn to land for shelter,
riding on the swell.

The curling waves come rolling in,
it is a wondrous sight.
If I could only paint them,
and get the movement right.

A massive wave comes crashing down,
as it hits upon a rock.
Then rises high into the air,
as the streams of spume unlock.

Tomorrow is another day,
the ocean may be calm.
And the stillness of the water,
will heal our souls like balm.

# The Butterfly

Who could make
this wondrous thing.
Such brilliant colours
on gossamer wing.

The symmetry of pattern,
as it flies from flower to flower.
Its tiny wings, fantastic,
with that amount of power.

No paint box could ever hold,
that amount of hues.
Of orange, yellows, purples,
scarlet, pinks and blues.

No-one could ever stamp it,
made-by-hand.
For this one's creator
is never from this land.

It drinks nectar
from the cherry trees.
The buddleia and the lilac,
it shares them with the bees.

Giving pleasure in our gardens,
every single year.
Life would never be the same,
if it failed to appear.

# A Perfect World

Lots more tolerance.
No more hate.
Kindness served
upon a plate.

No more wars.
No more greed.
Enough food
for the world to feed.

Peace and tranquillity.
Sympathy and care.
Plenty for all,
enough for us to share.

With wildlife all around us,
the songbirds and the bees,
we're halfway to perfection,
with the beauty of our trees.

# Our Wonderful Trees

Some branches of the old fir tree,
have now become quite bare.
But we still get so much pleasure,
watching squirrels playing there.

The little ones play chasing,
at acrobatics they excel.
As they empty out the peanuts,
for they know this food store well.

The mahonia keeps its berries,
where the blackbirds like to feed.
While little robin redbreast,
looks for grubs, instead of seed.

The pigeons are quite happy,
perching on the gate.
And rustling all the branches,
trying to attract a mate.

Witch hazel with its scented flowers,
in winter brings some cheer.
With yellow flowers and stamens red,
at the start of every year.

The dogwood is not evergreen,
sports red branches 'gainst the sky.
The berries are inedible,
but made lamp oil years gone by.

Eucalyptus with their scented leaves
a shade of silvery-green
Are used in flower arrangements,
and in florist shops are seen.

There are thousands of trees to cherish,
for those we all hold dear.
We must teach the children to value them,
Before they disappear.

Our wonderful trees,
and glorious shrubs,
keep feeding our birds,
with insects and grubs.

# To the Littlest One

Oh, tiny little violet,
peeping through the grass.
Last year there were just a few,
This year's bounty, there's a mass.

Tiny little violet,
your petals were all curled.
Now the sun has warmed you,
your petals have unfurled.

Tiny little violet,
if you could only talk.
You'd ask those human beings,
not to tread on you, and walk
around you,
not upon your head.
Your beauty they can't see,
or they would tip-toe round instead.

Mother Nature cares,
so never have a fear.
You're tiny but resilient,
you'll be back again next year.

# Free Gifts For All

The Bluebells nod their pretty heads,
in the shade beneath the trees.
While tiny violets peeping through
the grass are sure to please.

The blackbirds give us pleasure,
as their tuneful song they sing.
We've missed hearing them all winter,
but now it's turned to spring.

The robin's singing sweetly,
as he hopes to find a mate.
Oh, there she is, she's heard him.
She's now perched upon the gate.

The sun is warm, the sky is blue,
I'm sure you will all agree.
That all these treasures we enjoy,
Are precious, and they're FREE.

# Pets and other Poems

# The Old Straw Hat

The old straw hat that I once wore,
hangs neglected on the old barn door.
The pleasure it gave me for many hours,
changing the trimmings with ribbons and flowers.

I thought its usefulness was done.
My days were past, sitting in the sun.
Just as I thought it was past its best,
a robin decided to make its nest.

Even old hats can be useful things,
till fledglings start to use their wings.
It sports a deep and comfy crown,
lined with twigs and softest down.

If my hat could raise a smile,
it's had its uses for a while.
And if for its family it should yearn,
maybe next year they will return.

# The Downing Street Cat

My name is Larry, I'm out to impress,
as I live at a very important address.
I'm brushed and I'm combed to a very high sheen,
I'm on show to the public, so they keep me pristine.

When I meow at the door, it gets opened for me.
The cameras all click as the crowd smiles with glee.
Being perfectly groomed, down the steps I will sail,
as I wave to the crowds with my soft furry tail.

When I've had enough of the noise of the crowd,
I will climb up the steps and meow really loud.
For the doorman to open my well-known front door,
Saying thank you, I'll purr as I roll on the floor.

My owners keep changing every few years.
So I'm quite independent, wasting very few tears.
Not allowed in the boardroom - upon my soul,
I think they're afraid I'll turn into a mole.

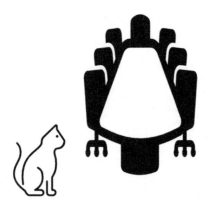

# Dumb Animal – Not Me

While sitting in my comfy chair,
I've found some time that's free.
My dog appeared from I know not where,
and a ball rolled off my knee.

Two loving eyes looked up at me.
They said, you've time to play.
You do not need that cup of tea,
we could Sit and Fetch and Stay.

I rolled the ball across the floor,
for Bonnie to retrieve.
She wagged her tail in thanks for more,
her craft and guile we can't believe.

Playing on the carpet,
really is a bore.
So she goes to fetch her nice new lead,
Our Not-So-Dumb Labrador.

## The Value of our Pets

I'm the most important one,
for I get taken walks.

No Polly is the clever one.
she whistles and she talks.

I never do a stroke of work,
but swim around all day.
And watch my owner teach the dog,
to sit and beg and stay.

The rabbit is quite clever,
as it hops instead of run.

And comes out for a carrot,
or some lettuce, or a bun.

But pussy is the clever one,
for food she's never late.

She laps her milk so daintily,
eats chicken off a plate.

When the day is cold she'll be
first through the cat flap.

Purring with contentment,
and ready for a nap.

She thinks which humans sitting down,
with warm and cosy knee.

That I can use to curl up tight,
and dream and just be me.

# The Joy of Bookshop Browsing

If ever I am lonely,
I know I can depend,
upon my local bookshop,
where I'll always find a friend.

There'll be memories from my childhood,
where my love of books began.
With Robin Hood, who helped the good,
and his friend Maid Marian.

Peter Pan and Wendy,
and Nana their faithful dog.
Beatrix Potter's Peter Rabbit,
Jeremy Fisher, the musical frog.

Tom the Water Baby,
who used to be a sweep.
Mrs Do-as-you-would-be-done-by,
memories we'll always keep.

Mabel Lucie Attwell's,
illustrations made us smile.
She will always be remembered,
for her drawings would beguile.

Charles Dickens's Christmas Carol,
brings characters to life.
Who could resist Oliver Twist,
Mr Micawber and his wife.

Poems by Rossetti and Keats,
and books by Patience Strong.
Wordsworth, Shelley and Browning,
all in my memory belong.

But all those life-time memories,
are always there to last.
Are brought back by these bookshelves,
the magic of the past.

# The Dentist Check-up Time Again

Check-up time comes round again,
I'll go at half-past eight.
Luckily, I've had no pain,
so won't get in a state.

Please go there and take a chair,
the Dentist won't be long.
We sit in a line, I'm feeling fine,
so nothing should go wrong.

It's my turn now, I don't know how,
my nerves seem all on edge.
He takes my coat, my hat, my bag,
and puts them on a ledge.

Head back please and open wide,
we'll see what we can find inside.
Ah, just one cavity, nurse McTavity,
holes like this we can't abide.

Please sit still, I'll get the drill.
He makes a bigger hole.
And then in haste, makes up the paste,
and shapes it in a roll.

Then a dentist's trick that makes me sick.
Some questions he will ask.
With a mouthful of tool, one feels such a fool,
when given such a task.

Just one wince, and one quick rinse,
I never felt much pain.
But six months more and what a bore,
it's check-up time again!

# I would like to be an Artist

With my paint box at the ready,
and my easel standing by,
I'll start with something simple,
A tree?  A rock?  A sky?


I need some inspiration.
I really want to paint,
but I need an easy subject.
Something pretty, something quaint.


I'm sitting on the clifftop,
with easel, paint and board.
With pallet knife and brushes,
the best I could afford.


The trickle of the sea,
as it creeps along the sand.
Or maybe two small children,
walking hand in hand.

The sand dunes look inviting,
with the sea pinks peeping through.
The sky of grey is lightening
to a lovely shade of blue.

Oh dear, the weather's changing.
It's coming on to rain.
But I'll come back here tomorrow,
And I'll PAINT—not DREAM again.

## Busy Christmas

The lights on the tree are shining brightly,
the children have dressed it so well.
Carols on the radio played twice nightly,
From the kitchen drifts a wonderful smell.

There's a secretive smile on everyone's face.
Presents to wrap, and more cards to write.
People have moved on, so old friends to trace.
Parties to plan – who should we invite?

The list on the wall is getting quite short,
I'm pleased I've been able to cope.
Without getting stressed, and not overwrought.
A New Year looms, which fills me with hope.

I'm taking the 'To do list' off the wall,
and wish Happy New Year to one and all.

## Out For Tea

A girl from the district of Bramwich,
ordered some tea and a sandwich.
But when she sat down,
she started to frown,
her expression had now changed to anguish.

The waitress while wiping the table,
was watching her reading the label.
She looked for the arrow,
but the space was too narrow,
the wrapping, she couldn't disable.

Her rare visits for tea were bi-annual,
next time she'd bring her brother Nathaniel.
Not to be woe begone,
they'd order a scone,
and bring a packaging manual.

# The Art Gallery

I'm walking round the gallery,
admiring all the art.
There are rural scenes by Constable,
and that is just the start.

There are paintings of Monet's Garden,
with delicate blossoms in Spring.
With Joshua Reynolds and Paul Gauguin,
one hardly knows where to begin.

Botticelli's Birth of Venus.
Sunsets and ships, William Turner.
Paintings of horses and dogs by George Stubbs,
to inspire the art loving learner.

There are beautiful paintings by Gainsborough,
William Hogarth and Renoir as well.
But no time to see more, we must head for the door,
as we hear the closing time bell.

## Time Flies

The list on the wall
says **THINGS TO DO**.
I can't do them all,
but I'll do just a few.

I feel enthusiastic,
and I'll do my best.
I'll tick off two or three,
then I'll have a rest.

A cup of tea nearly always
does the trick.
Then I'll carry on with jobbing,
as the clock goes tick.

I'm enjoying the challenge,
as the list starts to shrink.
But the day is flying by,
and I'm starting to think.

I must have a Gremlin,
living in my clock.
Moving the hands forward,
as it goes tick-tock

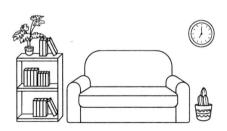

## Market Day

The pavements round the market,
throbbed with busy feet.
With customers both young and old,
looking for tasty things to eat.

The stallholders come to sell their wares,
each week in rain or sun.
For a small group in the corner,
the bargaining has begun.

Old Jenny with her bric-a-brac,
and curtain stall close by.
It was a weekly meeting place,
they hope it will stay dry.

The household stall is popular,
with gadgets, pots and pans.
The jolly smiling owner,
has many weekly fans.

They've had a friendly gossip,
The shopping now is done.
Just time to find a café,
for a coffee and a bun.

# The Reluctant Guest

I'm dressed up in my party frock,
with ribbons in my hair.
I'm waiting now for three o'clock,
there'll be children everywhere.

Mummy says I must be nice,
I didn't want to come.
Must be polite and smile a lot,
and must not suck my thumb.

I have a birthday present,
for little Sarah-Jane.
But I hate her younger brother,
he always is a pain.

As we arrive at half past three,
and knock upon the door.
The grown-ups smile and take our coats.
It really is a bore.

My coat and hat are on the hook.
My little bag is hung.
I see Johnny Brown across the room,
he's sticking out his tongue!

I must look out for Sarah-Jane,
and give her this little book.
I hope that she will like it,
when she has time to have a look.

Sticking the tail on the donkey and forfeits.
Pass the parcel and musical chairs.
Oranges and lemons, and blind man's buff,
and guessing games played in pairs.

Then it's tea-time at last,
with sandwiches and cake.
With jelly and ice cream and trifle,
which proved to be a mistake.

Johnny Brown was greedy,
ate three helpings very quick.
Then had to leave the table,
as he wanted to be sick.

We played more games, I felt so tired,
I didn't want to cry.
But felt so lonely for my Mum,
don't they know that I am shy?

Just then the front door opened,
and Auntie called my name.
I put on my hat and coat and shoes,
I'm glad my Mummy came.

I could hear singing and more music,
and such a lot of noise.
As I waved goodbye with a smile,
to the rest of the girls and boys.

Mummy smiled and asked me,
Did you have a lovely time?
'Oh yes,' I said. 'It was very nice.'
Is a white lie such a crime?

## No Quick Fix

The shopping was tiring,
I needed a drink.
A café was near,
so what do you think?
I entered the door,
found a table for one.
I went up to the counter,
and ordered a scone.

The assistant who served me,
was patient and kind.
Would I answer some questions,
just a few would I mind?
One shot or two?
Was she hiding a gun?
I then understood,
I must join in the fun.

Would I like filter or latte,
in a cup or a mug?
Skimmed milk or cream,
in my cup or a jug?
Would I like frothy,
or would I like flat?
The tables were polished,
would I please use a mat.

My coffee was ordered,
I was dying of thirst.
Would I return to my table,
I'd then be the first
that the waitress would serve
the table quite soon.
I needed that coffee,
I might have wished for the moon.

I only wanted a drink,
if I'd just been aware,
that it required
a full questionnaire.
Next time I go shopping,
I'll go with my daughter.
Who always carries
some sparkling Spring Water.

## My Day

I stubbed my toe upon the bed.
Not just bruised, but how it bled.

A pile of post was on the floor.
All junk mail, oh what a bore.

I was expecting just one letter.
I thought this day must get better.

I burnt the toast, I dropped a glass.
I thought this blighted day will pass.

It did. I met a lady when out walking.
I smiled at her. We started talking.

She said, your smile has made my day.
All my troubles fled away.

My day improved, I've made a friend.
No knowing how this day will end.

# Good Friends

They say good friends are hard to find.
I'm saying this with you in mind.

The hours you lend two listening ears.
We share our dreams. We share our fears.

We share the good times and the bad.
And try to comfort when we're sad.

We share our worries, laugh a lot.
We're glad we haven't lost the plot.

So as you turn another page,
look forward to another age.

We plan for better things ahead,
to live in hope, instead of dread.

And when we share a cup that cheers.
We can reminisce on happier years.

## Slimmer of the Month

I thought that I would diet,
to lose a stone or two.
I knew I ought to try it,
with a portly friend I knew.

We armed ourselves with helpful books
on calorie counting meals.
We kept the carbs and sugar low,
and you know how hard that feels!

My plate was full of lettuce leaves,
the meat was very lean.
Everything was very sparse.
Everything was green!

We weren't allowed a biscuit,
some chocolate or a crisp.
Oh pretty please, I'd like some cheese.
Alright then, just a wisp.

I'm weary and I'm hungry.
What can I eat that's nice?
I want to eat. I need a treat.
Some apple – just a slice?

Then the day of reckoning,
a month has now gone by.
I bet those scales could tell some tales,
of spirits low and high.

I hold my breath, I'm on the scales.
I don't feel any thinner.
Well, I'll be bound, I've lost a pound,
I'll go and have some dinner.

# Behind the Scenes at a Charity Shop

Sorting out the bags and bales,
the volunteers work well.
There's lots of waste that won't make sales.
Good quality items always sell.

We sort the clothes out in their size,
some have to go to waste.
We sometimes get a nice surprise,
good styles to suit the modern taste.

Curtains, cushions, table mats.
Slippers, scarves and shoes.
Dresses, jackets, coats and hats.
We sort, no time to lose.

A lady brought a massive sack.
She says she's going to move.
She has this load of bric-a-brac,
and hopes we will approve.

We find a box upon the floor,
been packed with fond affection.
A note on top says, there'll be more,
this was my china shoe collection.

A box of bricks, a teddy bear.
A tea-set just for two.
A well-loved doll that's got no hair.
A jigsaw, boxed, brand new.

We never know what we will find,
it's rewarding and it's fun.
And now we leave it all behind,
our three-hour shift is done.

## In the Gallery: Also known as the gods

A seat in the gallery,
is my monthly treat.
But goodness knows how many shows,
I've shared with the elite.

There are frescos on the ceiling,
also on the walls.
Where angels beguile with their comforting smile,
patrons miss all this from the stalls.

The gallery is warm in winter,
as the heat rises up from below.
How many plods from foyer to gods?
I'm too breathless, so I'll never know.

The lights they have dimmed,
to no more than a glow.
The gallery I've praised, and the curtain is raised.
I can now enjoy watching the show.

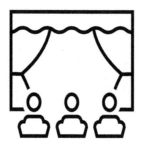

# A Magic Carpet

If I had a magic carpet,
what a blessing that would be.
I would climb upon it,
and float above the sea.

I'd see all the spring colours
of the countryside.
I'd soar up with the seagulls,
when they come in with the tide.

If I had a magic carpet,
it would be so quick.
But whatever am I thinking of?
I AM TRAVEL SICK.

## Poor Old Ben

Old Ben could be found sitting on a log,
with constant companion Bruce, his faithful dog.
Ben didn't beg, he didn't gripe,
but just sat there and smoked his pipe.

The residents of Canning Lea,
would bring his food, and mugs of tea.
He'd sometimes sit upon the stile,
but always had that winsome smile.

He sometimes had a tale to tell,
of times gone by, drawing water from the well.
Of horse drawn carts, with sacks of coal.
Of draymen dropping barrels down a hole.

Hot cross buns delivered in a van,
and for lighting, came the paraffin man.
Then one day Ben was there no more,
a sign went up on his caravan door.

I was happy here in Canning Lea,
The people were so kind to me.
I've left a gift of a million pounds,
to fund two recreation grounds.

## The Umbrella

The umbrella called a *Brolly* and a *Gamp,*
keeps our clothes from getting damp.
Keeps us comfortable, keeps us dry,
when heavens open in the sky.

The coloured ones, to us bring cheer,
when wet and dreary days appear.
I've one in red and one in 'yeller.'
I was very fond of my umbrella.

While walking on the esplanade,
the wind blew up and I'm afraid.
My umbrella then turned inside-out,
now holds enough water for next year's drought!

# Christmas Celebration

Christmas can't be cancelled,
two years in a row.
So, we are going to celebrate,
a gig we're going to throw.

Up will go the streamers,
Christmas trees we'll light.
'Cos we are going to celebrate,
late into the night.

With family we will party,
and Grandma gets a hug.
The youngsters strumming their guitars,
the rest all cut a rug.

The wine will flow like water.
The dancers take to the floor.
They feel alive and start to jive.
The audience plead for more.

So Christmas won't be cancelled,
We're going to have a gig.
And we are going to celebrate,
And celebrate it B-I-G.

## Perfection – New Baby

The miracle of a baby,
as it slips from its cocoon.
And starts to breathe our oxygen,
we shall hear it very soon.

A little cry, 'I'm here at last,
I'll make my presence known.
I'll need your love each hour, each day,
until I'm fully grown.'

On inspection we will see,
ten tiny fingers, also toes,
Ten perfectly formed fingernails,
shell like ears and cutest nose.

The skin like velvet,
softest down.
The head with its very
delicate crown.

You've many sleepless nights ahead,
you'll get worried, you'll get stressed.
With that precious life to share your love,
you'll know you're truly blessed.

## Unknown Destination

Where will it lead,
this winding lane.
Is it contentment,
or will it be pain?

Will it be good,
or will it be bad?
Will it be happy,
or will it be sad?

Do we welcome the choice,
or do we ignore it?
Do we heed good advice,
or do we abhor it?

Self-discipline,
is our very best friend.
It protects us from trouble,
as we turn round that bend.

## Life's Challenges

When you're feeling sad and lonely,
and your troubles overwhelm.
Remember that the boat you're sailing,

you are at the helm.
Each problem, treat them one by one,
not as an impossible pile.
Keep your sense of humour,
and try to raise a smile.

A positive attitude you must have,
for it will get you through.
Grey clouds will surely fade away,
and the sky will turn to blue.

# The Isle of Wight

Are you looking for contentment,
where the pace of life is slow?
A place to find a little peace,
there is one that I know.

With lovely beaches, countryside,
with downs perfect to walk.
The residents are friendly,
with time to smile and talk.

There's Gurnard with its sunsets,
admired throughout the land.
Ventnor Botanic gardens,
Alum Bay with coloured sand.

So if you need a holiday,
if you're nervy and uptight.
I suggest with confidence,
you try the **ISLE OF WIGHT**.

Printed in Great Britain
by Amazon